I LiKE tHE Cats

Words & Pictures
by P.J. Peregrine

ISBN: 1722037075

for Tulia Grace Siviglia

I love all cats, scruffy or sleek,
Feisty or finicky, bold or meek.

BISTRO
Benjamin

Cats that cuddle, cats that purr.

Cats with very fluffy fur.

LE MARCHÉ

Cats dressed up with stripe or splotch.
Cats that sit up high and watch.

Patisserie de Paris
Ouvert
Lavande

Cats that strike a regal pose.

Cats that lick me on my nose.

Cats that hide and cats that nap.

Cats that curl up in my lap.

Cats that saunter, cats that pace.

Cats that slink and pounce and chase.

Cats that drape and cats that dangle.

Cats that can't resist a tangle.

Cats that lounge out in the sun.
Cats that follow when I run.

Every cat is simply fine.

But my favorite cat is mine.

Hi, I'm Simka, the author's cat. She asked me to tell you how to treat a kitty. Are you ready?

Please be kind and show you like me.
Never pull my tail or strike me.

← Carry me like this, not that! →
I'm not a toy. I am a cat!

Don't give me a chicken bone,
Grapes and chocolate make me moan.

I think playing rough is crummy.
Please don't ever touch my tummy.

Play with me, but do not tease me.
Big, loud noises do not please me.

If I'm frightened, I might hide.
When I trust, I'm by your side.

I'm your friend. I'll show you love.
Just your kindness is enough.

Simka

Other Books by P.J. Peregrine

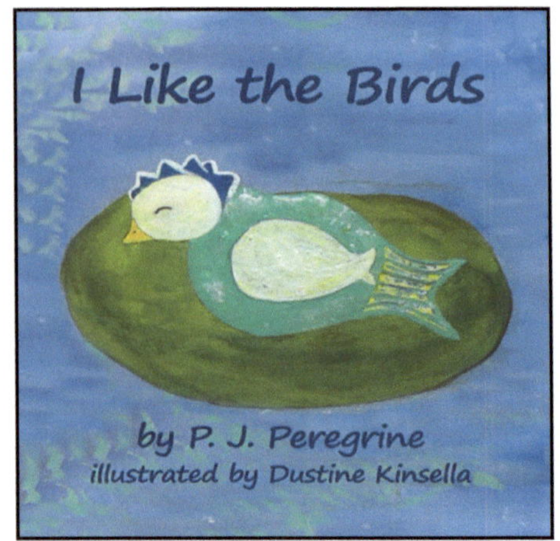

I Like the Birds
illustrated by Dustine Kinsella

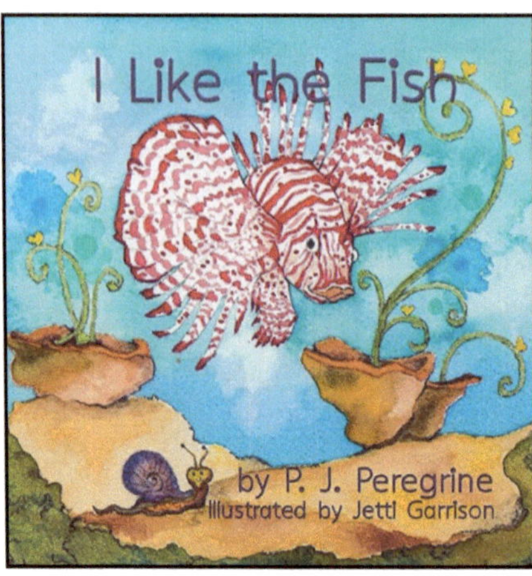

I Like the Fish
illustrated by Jetti Garrison

The Good Trade
illustrated by Jan Orsini

Mama Heidi Loves
illustrated by Theresa Dedmon

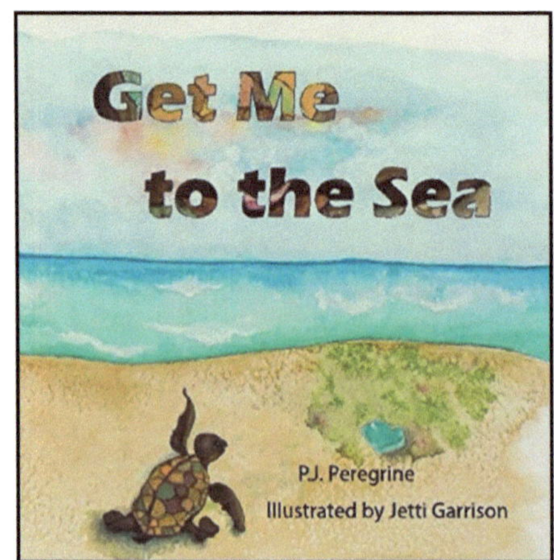

Get Me to the Sea
illustrated by Jetti Garrison
French edition also available, titled

Le Grand Voyage